North Dakota

by Rebecca Stromstad
Glaser

Consultant:
Kimberly K. Porter
Associate Professor
University of North Dakota
Grand Forks

Capstone
press
Mankato, Minnesota

Capstone Press
151 Good Counsel Drive • P.O. Box 669 • Mankato, Minnesota 56002
http://www.capstone-press.com

Library of Congress Cataloging-in-Publication Data
Glaser, Rebecca Stromstad.
   North Dakota / by Rebecca Stromstad Glaser.
   p. cm.—(Land of liberty)
   Includes bibliographical references and index.
   Contents: About North Dakota—Land, climate, and wildlife—History
of North Dakota—Government and politics—Economy and resources—People
and culture.
   ISBN 0-7368-2191-0 (hardcover)
   1. North Dakota—Juvenile literature. [1. North Dakota.] I. Title. II. Series.
F636.3.G58 2004
978.4—dc21
                                      2003000080

Summary: An introduction to the geography, history, government, politics,
   economy, resources, people, and culture of North Dakota, including maps,
   charts, and a recipe.

Editorial Credits
Christopher Harbo, editor; Jennifer Schonborn, series designer; Linda Clavel, book
   designer; Enoch Peterson, illustrator; Kelly Garvin, photo researcher; Eric
   Kudalis, product planning editor

Photo Credits
Cover images: bison at Theodore Roosevelt National Park, Kent & Donna Dannen;
   rolling prairie near Jamestown, North Dakota, Houserstock/Jan Butchofsky

Bruce Coleman Inc./Gary Withey, 4; Bruce Coleman Inc./Robert Carr, 56; Capstone
Press/Gary Sundermeyer, 54; Corbis, 27; Corbis/Annie Griffiths Belt, 45; Corbis/Charles
E. Rotkin, 29; Corbis/Layne Kennedy, 63; Corbis Sygma/Scott Takushi, 31; Courtesy,
North Dakota Secretary of State, 55 (both); James P. Rowan, 1; North Dakota Tourism
Department, 53; North Wind Picture Archives/N. Carter, 12–13, 21; State Historical
Society of North Dakota/#A4245/#0941–12/#0823–04/#D0479/#0941–12, 23, 24–25,
37, 43, 58; Stock Montage Inc./The Newberry Library, 18; Tom Bean, 8, 14, 15, 17, 32,
38, 40–41, 42, 46, 52; University of North Dakota Athletic Media Relations, 50–51;
U.S. Postal Service, 59; Visuals Unlimited/R. Hutchison, 57

Artistic Effects
Comstock Klips, Corbis, PhotoDisc Inc.

**The author dedicates this book to her grandmother Bernice Stromstad, a longtime
North Dakota resident.**

1 2 3 4 5 6 08 07 06 05 04 03

Table of Contents

A flower garden surrounds a fountain at the International Peace Garden near Dunseith, North Dakota.

Chapter 1

About North Dakota

On the border between the United States and Canada lies a quiet place that honors peace. The border is the longest undefended border in the world. The International Peace Garden honors more than 150 years of peace between the United States and Canada.

Visitors to the Peace Garden first notice the colorful gardens with pools and fountains. A clock made of flowers sits on the side of a hill. Walking farther, visitors see the 100-foot (30-meter) pillars of the Peace Tower. Behind the Peace Tower is the Chapel of Peace, the only building in the world built across a national border. Quotations about peace are carved into the walls inside the chapel.

The Peace Garden State

The International Peace Garden gives North Dakota one of its nicknames. The phrase "Peace Garden State" has appeared on the state's license plates since 1956.

North Dakota is also known as the Flickertail State and the Roughrider State. The Flickertail State nickname comes from the Richardson ground squirrels in the state. The squirrel flicks its tail while running. The Roughrider State nickname comes from Theodore Roosevelt's Rough Riders. Roosevelt led this group of soldiers in the Battle of San Juan Hill during the Spanish-American War (1898). Some of the Rough Riders were from North Dakota.

North Dakota is in the north-central United States. The Canadian provinces of Saskatchewan and Manitoba border North Dakota on the north. On the east, the Bois de Sioux River and the Red River of the North separate North Dakota from Minnesota. South Dakota borders North Dakota to the south. Montana borders it on the west.

North Dakota Cities

CANADA

SASKATCHEWAN

MANITOBA

MONTANA

MINNESOTA

International Peace Garden ○

Pembina ●

● Rugby

● Minot

● Williston

Grand Forks ●

Red River of the North

NORTH DAKOTA

Medora ●

● Dickinson

Mandan ● ☆ Bismarck

● Jamestown

Fargo ●

Bois de Sioux River

SOUTH DAKOTA

N
W · E
S

Legend	
	American Indian Reservation
☆	Capital
●	City
○	Point of Interest
〜	River

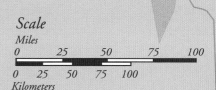

Scale
Miles
0   25   50   75   100

0   25   50   75   100
Kilometers

Prairie potholes cover central North Dakota. These shallow ponds were left behind by glaciers that melted thousands of years ago.

Chapter 2

Land, Climate, and Wildlife

Thousands of years ago, glaciers shaped much of North Dakota's land. The glaciers melted to form Lake Agassiz (AG-uh-see), which covered more than 110,000 square miles (284,900 square kilometers). In places, this giant lake was 300 feet (91 meters) deep. Today, the area once covered by Lake Agassiz is known as the Red River Valley.

North Dakota is part of two large land regions. The Central Lowlands cover eastern North Dakota. This region extends from the Great Plains in the west to the Appalachian Mountains in the east. The Great Plains cover western North Dakota. This large plains area extends from Texas into Canada.

The Central Lowlands

The Red River Valley in eastern North Dakota is part of the Central Lowlands. The Red River Valley was once the floor of glacial Lake Agassiz. The lake left the area full of rich soil, making it a good farming region. The Red River Valley is the flattest and lowest area of the state. The state's lowest point is in this region near Pembina. It is 750 feet (229 meters) above sea level.

The Drift Prairie covers central North Dakota. It is slightly higher than the Red River Valley. Glaciers left deposits of finely ground rock, sand, and gravel called drift in the area. The Drift Prairie has rolling hills and plains. Shallow ponds called prairie potholes, or sloughs, provide nesting areas for ducks and other birds. Forested hills called the Turtle Mountains stand along the Canadian border.

The Great Plains

In North Dakota, the Great Plains begin west of the Missouri Escarpment. The escarpment is a slope that rises between

North Dakota's Land Features

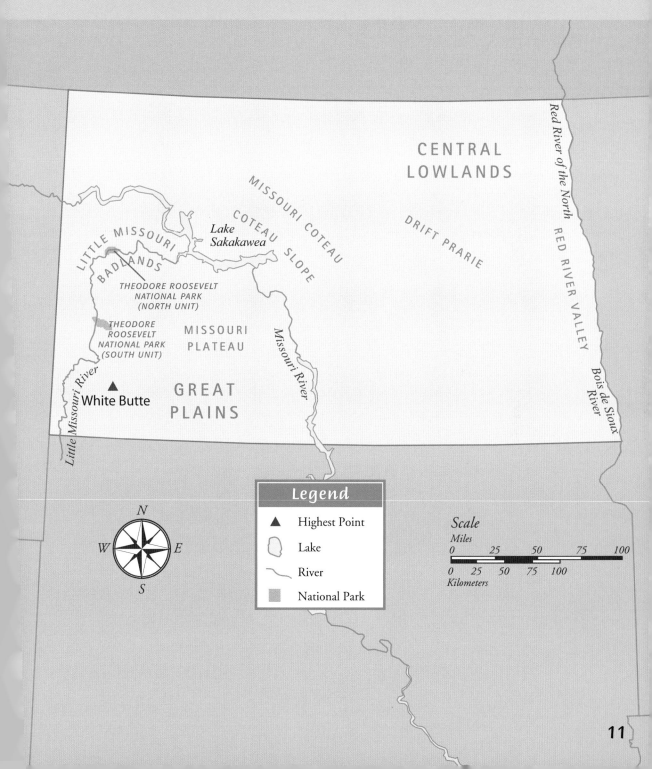

CENTRAL LOWLANDS

Red River of the North

RED RIVER VALLEY

DRIFT PRARIE

MISSOURI COTEAU

COTEAU SLOPE

Lake Sakakawea

LITTLE MISSOURI BADLANDS

THEODORE ROOSEVELT NATIONAL PARK (NORTH UNIT)

THEODORE ROOSEVELT NATIONAL PARK (SOUTH UNIT)

MISSOURI PLATEAU

Missouri River

GREAT PLAINS

Little Missouri River

▲ White Butte

Bois de Sioux River

Legend

▲ Highest Point

Lake

River

National Park

Scale

Miles

0   25   50   75   100

0   25   50   75   100

Kilometers

N W E S

600 and 800 feet (183 and 244 meters) above the surrounding land. Four smaller regions in the state are part of the Great Plains. They are the Missouri Coteau, the Coteau Slope, the Missouri Plateau, and the Little Missouri Badlands.

The Missouri Coteau and the Coteau Slope lie on the eastern edge of the Great Plains. Like the Drift Prairie, the Missouri Coteau has prairie potholes and many low, rolling hills. The Coteau Slope has slightly higher rolling hills.

The Missouri Plateau is the largest part of the Great Plains in North Dakota. Southwest of the Missouri River, the plateau has broad valleys, hills, and flat-topped hills called buttes.

West of the river, the land slopes higher, forming many buttes. White Butte is the highest point in the state. It rises 3,506 feet (1,069 meters) above sea level. The land in this region is drier than the rest of the state. Most ranchers in the Missouri Plateau use this drier land to raise cattle.

The Little Missouri Badlands lie along the Little Missouri River. The Badlands are covered with canyons, gorges, and buttes. Water erosion from rivers formed colorful buttes. Many buttes have visible layers of brick-red scoria rock and yellow, blue, and gray clays. Much of the Badlands are part of Theodore Roosevelt National Park.

The land of the Missouri Plateau rises gradually near White Butte. White Butte is the highest point in North Dakota.

Theodore Roosevelt National Park

Theodore Roosevelt came to the Badlands of the Dakota Territory in 1883 and started a ranch. Roosevelt grew to love North Dakota. He worried about the state's wildlife and land. When he became president, Roosevelt made many areas in the United States into national monuments.

After Roosevelt's death in 1919, many people wanted to honor him with a memorial. People had many ideas. Finally, a park was chosen. In 1947, Theodore Roosevelt National Memorial Park was created in western North Dakota. In 1978, the park's name changed to Theodore Roosevelt National Park.

The park has two sections, the North Unit and the South Unit. The North Unit has high buttes and forests. More plant life grows there than in the South Unit. The South Unit is filled with rocky buttes. Here, visitors see layers of different colored rocks.

Theodore Roosevelt National Park is home to many animals. Buffalo, elk, and bighorn sheep are common. Visitors often stop their cars to wait for a buffalo herd to cross the road. Smaller animals in the park include coyotes, red foxes, squirrels, and beavers. Small gopher-like animals called prairie dogs build homes underground.

Climate

In North Dakota, winter weather can last from November to April. Temperatures below 0 degrees Fahrenheit (minus 18 degrees Celsius) are common. Because North Dakota's land is mostly flat, winds rush across the state. In winter, high winds can cause even a light snowfall to turn into a blinding blizzard.

Halos sometimes appear in the sky on cold winter days in North Dakota. These halos of sunlight form when light reflects off ice particles in the air.

Winds can also bring warm, dry air to the state in winter. Chinook winds from the west often cause milder winters in the western part of the state.

Summer weather usually lasts from June to August in North Dakota. Summer is the season with the most rainfall. North Dakota receives an average of 8 inches (20 centimeters) of rain each summer. Most of the rain falls in the Red River Valley.

Plants and Wildlife

North Dakota's main plants are grasses. Before settlement, the land was covered with prairie grasses 6 feet (1.8 meters) high. Today, the tallest grasses grow in the Red River Valley. The grasses get shorter from east to west as rainfall decreases.

Wildflowers and shrubs are common in the state. The state flower is the wild rose. Sagebrush and other shrubs grow in the drier western part of the state.

Few trees grow in the state. Most of the state's trees grow along river valleys and in the Turtle Mountains.

Buffalo graze under cloudy skies in Theodore Roosevelt National Park.

North Dakota's wildlife population has decreased since settlement. Herds of buffalo once roamed North Dakota. Overhunting from the 1840s to the 1870s killed most of the buffalo. White-tailed deer and mule deer live throughout the state. Elk and antelope live in western North Dakota.

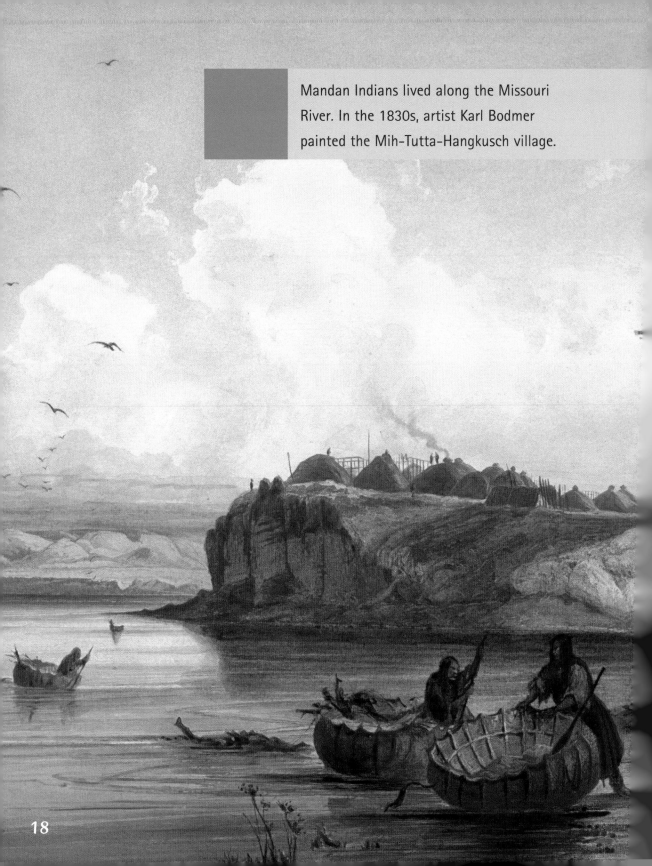

Mandan Indians lived along the Missouri River. In the 1830s, artist Karl Bodmer painted the Mih-Tutta-Hangkusch village.

Chapter 3

History of North Dakota

The Mandan Indians were the first people to settle in North Dakota. From about 1350 to the mid-1600s, they lived along the Missouri River in earth lodge villages. The Mandan farmed and hunted buffalo and elk.

By the mid-1600s, other Indian tribes began moving into the area. The Hidatsa and the Arikara Indians settled near the Mandan. The Ojibwa, also called the Chippewa, pushed the Dakota Indians from Minnesota to North Dakota. One group of Ojibwa moved west from Minnesota and settled in the Turtle Mountains. The Dakota, Nakota, and Lakota Indians lived in tepees and moved from place to place. These three tribes were later called the Sioux. The Cheyenne, Crow,

Cree, and Assiniboin Indians also moved in and out of the North Dakota area.

Explorations and Fur Trade

One of the first white men to come to North Dakota was a French fur trader named Pierre La Vérendrye. He visited the Mandan villages in December 1738. He watched the Mandan trade tobacco, buffalo hides, and corn for muskets, knives, axes, and kettles with the Assiniboin Indians.

During the 1700s, the British, Spanish, and French all tried to set up trade in North Dakota. European traders wanted fur pelts. Beaver pelts were the most valuable. They were used for making fur hats in Europe. Mink and otter also attracted early trappers.

Trade was not always good for the Indians. Because North Dakota was so far from most trading posts, Indians had to pay higher prices for goods. European traders also brought diseases. In the 1780s, smallpox killed many American Indians. Some tribes lost half their members.

Today, a reconstruction of Fort Mandan shows visitors what life was like for Lewis and Clark during the winter of 1804 to 1805.

Meriwether Lewis and William Clark were the most famous explorers to visit North Dakota. Lewis, Clark, and a group of about 30 men traveled up the Missouri River to explore the Louisiana Territory. President Thomas Jefferson bought this large area from France in 1803. Lewis and Clark reached Mandan villages in 1804. The group stopped there

for the winter and built Fort Mandan. At Fort Mandan, Lewis and Clark met Toussaint Charbonneau and hired him as an interpreter. His wife, Sacagawea, also spelled Sakakawea, joined the expedition as well. She helped the group trade for horses with her native tribe, the Shoshone.

After Lewis and Clark's expedition, more fur traders traveled to the North Dakota area. By the 1830s, Fort Union at the mouth of the Yellowstone River had become a center for fur trade.

Roads to Settlement

Until the mid-1800s, few people were interested in settling in North Dakota because traveling there was difficult. By 1860, traveling to the area became easier. Steamboats carried passengers and supplies up and down the Missouri River.

In 1861, the Dakota Territory was created. It included North Dakota, South Dakota, and parts of Wyoming and Montana. When gold was discovered in Montana, people began traveling through northern Dakota Territory.

In 1872, the Northern Pacific Railroad built tracks across the Red River. The railroad reached Bismarck by 1873. Railroads gave settlers an easy way to reach the area. They also brought supplies to the settlers.

Cheap land drew some settlers to North Dakota in the 1860s. The Homestead Act of 1862 gave 160 acres (65 hectares)

In 1879, workers at Sweet Briar Cut, west of Bismarck, dug a pass for the Northern Pacific Railroad.

of land to anyone who would farm it for five years. Settlers could also buy cheap land from the railroads. The railroads encouraged settlers to plant wheat crops. The railroads could then make money by transporting the wheat to eastern states.

Population Boom

North Dakota's population boomed in the late 1800s. From 1878 to 1890, the population grew from 16,000 to 191,000. Many people came to the Red River Valley to grow wheat.

Investors from other states built huge corporate farms called bonanza farms. Some of these farms were as large as 75,000 acres (30,000 hectares). Each farm used hundreds of work animals, machines, and seasonal workers. One bonanza farm could use as many as 195 reapers, 53 binders, and 400 workers during the harvest season. Periods of good rainfall and weather made the farms productive and profitable.

In western North Dakota, land was better for grazing cattle. Investors from other states built bonanza ranches there.

In the late 1800s and early 1900s, the wheat harvest was called "threshing time." North Dakota's bonanza farms hired many workers to help during threshing time.

"Dakota is a great land for extremes, either too hot or too cold, too wet or too dry."

—Mary Dodge Woodward, sister-in-law of a bonanza farm owner

In 1881, General James E. Brisban published a book called *The Beef Bonanza: or How to Get Rich on the Plains.* This book attracted many cattle ranchers to the state.

As the population grew, people wanted to have more control over their government. The U.S. Congress appointed all the officials for territories. North Dakota gained statehood in 1889. That same year, South Dakota, Montana, and Washington also became states.

Early 1900s

The early 1900s were years of growth for North Dakota. Between 1900 and 1915, the population grew 135 percent. Farmers sold crops for good prices. They tried growing new crops including flaxseed, oats, barley, and hay. Flaxseed is used to make oils for food and medicine.

Some industry developed in western North Dakota in the early 1900s. Brick-making factories made use of the state's clay deposits. Lignite coal was discovered in the western part of the state. Lignite produces less sulfur than other types of coal when it burns.

Depressions and World War II

In the 1920s, the price of wheat dropped. U.S. farmers were raising more wheat than was needed. In 1923, banks went out of business. North Dakota entered a depression.

After the stock market crashed in 1929, the whole country entered the Great Depression (1929–1939). North Dakota suffered more than many other states. Drought, winds, and

During the Great Depression, many North Dakota farmers and their families struggled to survive years of crop failures and poor prices.

grasshoppers damaged crops, especially in the west.

During the Great Depression, the federal government started programs to help U.S. citizens. North Dakota received $142 million from the federal government between 1933 and 1940. Federal aid programs gave jobs and money to people who could not earn a living.

The aid programs helped, but many farmers lost their farms in the 1930s. Eventually, higher prices for crops during World War II (1939–1945) helped to pull North Dakota out of the Great Depression.

Postwar Years

North Dakota's economy grew after World War II. In 1951, oil was discovered near Tioga in western North Dakota. In 1954, the federal government built air bases near Minot and Grand Forks. The air bases brought more people to the state.

In 1953, the Garrison Dam was completed. This dam provides hydroelectric power for the state. The dam also created a reservoir named Lake Sakakawea. The lake is

The Garrison Dam holds back the water of the Missouri River to create Lake Sakakawea.

about 180 miles (290 kilometers) long. It has become a large recreation area for people who like to fish, water-ski, or sail.

In 1972, the United States made a deal to sell more grain to the former Soviet Union. Wheat exports from the United States doubled. The large demand for grain increased prices. North Dakota wheat farmers made profits. They also went into debt as they bought more machinery and land. Later when prices dropped again, farmers were unable to pay their debts. Many farmers went out of business.

Recent Challenges

The weather continues to be a challenge for North Dakota. In 1988, the state suffered a severe drought. Many farmers lost money.

Between 1996 and 1997, the Red River Valley had one of the worst winters on record. Eight blizzards hit the area from November 1996 to April 1997. The large amounts of snowfall caused huge floods in the spring.

The city of Grand Forks was hit the hardest. People in Grand Forks built dikes and walls with sandbags. They hoped the sandbags would protect them if the Red River rose to 52 feet (15.8 meters). The river rose to 54 feet (16.5 meters), putting much of the town under water. People had to leave their homes. National Guard troops were called in to help. When Grand Forks residents returned after the flood, many of their homes had been damaged. Some homes had to be torn down.

In April 1997, floodwaters from the Red River of the North covered buildings, bridges, and streets in Grand Forks and East Grand Forks, Minnesota.

North Dakota's capitol is the tallest building in the state. It rises 19 stories above Bismarck.

Government and Politics

When North Dakota first became a state, many people did not trust government. Some Dakota Territory politicians had cheated people out of money. Many people were afraid railroads and grain mills would try to control the government.

North Dakota's constitution shows these fears. When it was first written, the constitution was six times longer than the U.S. Constitution. It limited the power of the governor and the legislature. It also created several state-owned institutions. These include a university, an agricultural college, two teachers' colleges, and a school of forestry. A veterans' home, schools for the blind and deaf, and a state hospital for the mentally ill were also built. Most of these institutions still

Did you know...?

Both North Dakota and South Dakota became states on November 2, 1889. When President Benjamin Harrison signed the papers for statehood, he mixed them up to keep their order secret. No one knows which state gained statehood first. North Dakota is listed first as 39th because it comes first in the alphabet.

exist today. They cannot be easily closed because they were set up in the constitution.

Branches of Government

North Dakota's government has executive, legislative, and judicial branches. The governor is the head of the executive branch. Governors are elected to four-year terms. The governor signs or vetoes laws passed by both houses of the legislature.

North Dakota's legislative branch is called the legislative assembly. It has a house of representatives and a senate. Representatives serve two-year terms and senators serve four-year terms. The legislature meets four months in odd-numbered years.

North Dakota's judicial branch has three levels. At the lowest level, municipal courts hear cases about city laws. District courts are the main trial courts in the state. Each of the state's 53 counties has a district court. District courts hear criminal, civil, and juvenile cases.

North Dakota's State Government

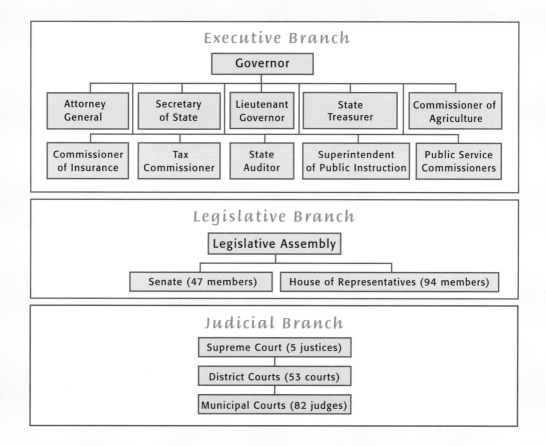

Executive Branch

Governor

- Attorney General
- Secretary of State
- Lieutenant Governor
- State Treasurer
- Commissioner of Agriculture
- Commissioner of Insurance
- Tax Commissioner
- State Auditor
- Superintendent of Public Instruction
- Public Service Commissioners

Legislative Branch

Legislative Assembly

- Senate (47 members)
- House of Representatives (94 members)

Judicial Branch

- Supreme Court (5 justices)
- District Courts (53 courts)
- Municipal Courts (82 judges)

The supreme court is the highest court in the state. It hears appeals from the district courts. Five justices sit on the state supreme court. The chief justice is elected by the supreme court justices and the district judges in the state.

When the supreme court has too many cases, it can give some of them to a temporary court of appeals. Three judges make up the court of appeals.

Recall, Initiative, and Referendum

Even 30 years after statehood, North Dakotans still did not trust government. In 1919, the power of recall was added to the constitution. Recall lets people petition for elected officials to be removed from office. That same year, initiative and referendum were made easier for people to use. Initiative lets voters put a new law on a ballot without going through the state legislature. Referendum lets people vote on laws already passed by the state legislature.

In 1921, members of the Independent Voters Association (IVA) party used the power of recall. The party disagreed with the way elected officials were running state businesses. The party petitioned for the recall of the governor, attorney general, and the commissioner of agriculture and labor. An election was held, and the IVA candidates won all three offices. This was the first time in U.S. history that state elected officials were recalled.

Nonpartisan League

In the early 1900s, many North Dakotans wanted the state government to control more businesses. They believed that private businesses controlled too much of the politics in the state. People thought the state government should control banking and insurance. They believed state-run businesses would be able to give people lower costs and better services.

These thoughts led to the formation of the Nonpartisan League (NPL). A. C. Townley (at left) started this political party in 1915. Farmers who were getting low prices for their crops liked his ideas. The NPL wanted state ownership of grain elevators, flour mills, and packing plants. It also supported state-sponsored hail insurance and state-owned banks.

In 1916, NPL candidates won the elections for almost every state office. While in office, the NPL members established the State Bank of North Dakota, the State Mill and Elevator, and a state hail insurance program. The bank, the mill and elevator, and the insurance program still are in business today.

A farmer uses a combine to harvest a row of wheat. The combine separates the wheat grains from the stalks.

Chapter 5

Economy and Resources

North Dakota is known for its good farmland and large cattle ranches. But agriculture is not the state's only source of income. Coal mining and oil drilling also help North Dakota's economy. In recent years, the state's medical and financial service industries helped the state grow.

Agriculture

One of North Dakota's biggest natural resources is its rich, fertile soil. This resource has made agriculture the most important part of the state's economy since statehood.

North Dakota farmers grow many crops. Wheat is the leading crop in the state. Most farmers grow hard red spring wheat. This variety is good for making flour used in bread, bagels, and hard rolls. Farmers also grow durum wheat, a type of hard wheat used for making pasta. North Dakota farmers produce 73 percent of the nation's durum wheat. Farmers also grow sugar beets, potatoes, soybeans, sunflowers, barley, and flaxseed.

Farmers and ranchers also raise livestock. Cattle and sheep are the most common farm animals. Milk, beef, and wool are the most widely produced livestock products in the state.

North Dakota's manufacturing industries are tied to agriculture. Six pasta plants make pasta from the durum

wheat grown in the state. Case International makes four-wheel drive tractors in Fargo. American Crystal Sugar processes sugar beets into sugar in factories in Hillsboro and Drayton.

Mining

Another natural resource in North Dakota is lignite coal. Western North Dakota has the largest known single deposit of lignite coal in the world. About 350 billion tons (318 billion metric tons) of lignite coal lie underground. Four mining operations mine coal for electric plants in the state.

Ranchers drive cattle across a river in western North Dakota.

A well pumps oil south of Medora.

Oil and natural gas are also found in western North
Dakota. Most of the oil is drilled in the Williston Basin.
North Dakota is the ninth largest oil producing state.
It produced 33 million barrels of oil in 2000. Natural gas is
processed at nine plants.

Harold Schafer

Harold Schafer is one of North Dakota's most famous business owners. He was born on a small farm near Stanton in 1912. His family moved often. Even as a young child, Harold took many jobs to earn money. After high school, he worked as a traveling salesperson for various companies in North Dakota.

In 1942, Schafer began selling Gold Seal Floor Wax. He started the business in his basement. He quit his job in Fargo and borrowed money to keep his new company going. Schafer's hard work paid off in 1948. His new product, Glass Wax, was sold nationally. Two other popular products he created were Snowy Bleach and Mr. Bubble, a bubble bath mix for kids.

Schafer was well known for his generosity. He helped develop the historic pioneer town of Medora. Schafer founded the Theodore Roosevelt Medora Foundation. This group operates many of the attractions in Medora that bring thousands of tourists to the state each year. Schafer died December 2, 2001.

Did you know...?
In the 1950s and 1960s, uranium was mined in North Dakota. Uranium is a radioactive metal used to create electricity at nuclear power plants.

Southwestern North Dakota has rich clay deposits. The clay is used for making bricks, pottery, and tile. Bentonite is a claylike material mined in southwestern North Dakota. Bentonite is used in soaps, cleaners, and cat litter.

Service Industries

In 2000, most of North Dakota's income came from service industries. Meritcare is a combined clinic and hospital based in Fargo. It is the largest employer in the state. In recent years, Meritcare has added several branch clinics in towns near Fargo.

Finance, insurance, and real estate are also important service industries in the state. These businesses made up about 16 percent of the state's income in 2000.

In 2000, income from government was about 14 percent of the state's economy. North Dakota has more than 70,000 state and federal government employees. Many federal government employees work at the air force bases near

Airmen work on a B-52 bomber at the U.S. Air Force base near Grand Forks.

Grand Forks and Minot. Many state government employees work at public schools and universities.

In 2001, Great Plains Software, a company in Fargo, was sold to Microsoft for $1.1 million. Great Plains Software is now a division of Microsoft Business Solutions. Microsoft Business Solutions still operates in Fargo. More than 900 people work there.

The Rinats Dancers of Minot wear Norwegian sweaters at the Norsk Høstfest in Minot.

People and Culture

Since the first Mandan Indians settled along the Missouri River, many people have come to North Dakota, and many have left. North Dakota has only 642,200 people living across 70,704 square miles (183,123 square kilometers) of land. Because of the small population, North Dakotans enjoy low crime rates and a friendly, small-town way of life.

Ethnic Groups

People with European backgrounds make up 91.7 percent of North Dakota's population. Most of these people are descended from the European settlers who came to the state in the 1800s. Many North Dakota settlers did not come

"North Dakota seems—and is—far from everything . . . Predictably, the people who inhabit such vast and lonely lands are a sturdy, tenacious lot, honest, thrifty, and proud."

—Neal R. Peirce, The Great Plains States of America, *1973*

directly from their home country. They settled in Michigan, Wisconsin, and Minnesota before moving west. Scandinavians are the state's largest group of European immigrants. They came from Norway, Sweden, Denmark, Finland, and Iceland. Germans and German-Russians are the second largest group. Many people can also trace their roots to French-Canadian, Irish, Scottish, or English settlers.

American Indians are the second largest ethnic group in North Dakota. American Indians make up 4.8 percent of the population. Most Indians in North Dakota live on the state's five reservations. The Ojibwa and Métis live on the Turtle Mountain Reservation in north-central North Dakota. The Métis people have a mixed heritage, usually with Ojibwa and French backgrounds.

The Mandan, Hidatsa, and Arikara, now called the Three Affiliated Tribes, live on the Fort Berthold Reservation in the western part of the state. Three other reservations are home to Dakota Indians. The Spirit Lake Reservation is near Devils

North Dakota's Ethnic Backgrounds

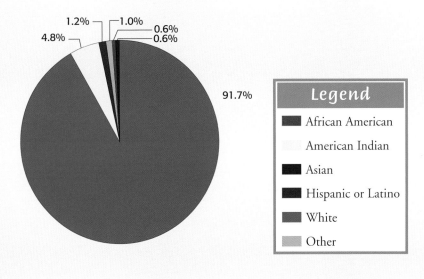

1.2% — 1.0%
0.6%
0.6%
4.8%
91.7%

Legend
■ African American
□ American Indian
■ Asian
■ Hispanic or Latino
■ White
■ Other

Lake in east-central North Dakota. The Standing Rock and Lake Traverse reservations cross the border between North Dakota and South Dakota.

A small percentage of North Dakota's population is Hispanic, African American, or Asian. Hispanics make up 1.2 percent of the population. African Americans and Asian Americans each make up less than 1 percent of North Dakota's population.

Sports and Pastimes

North Dakotans enjoy outdoor sports. The state is known as one of the best duck hunting regions. In winter, snowmobiling is popular. Many North Dakotans also enjoy birdwatching. The Chase Lake National Wildlife Refuge near Jamestown is the largest nesting ground for white pelicans in North America.

Although North Dakota does not have any pro sports, people enjoy watching the RedHawks, a minor league baseball team based in Fargo and Moorhead, Minnesota. North Dakota State University is known for its football team, the Bison.

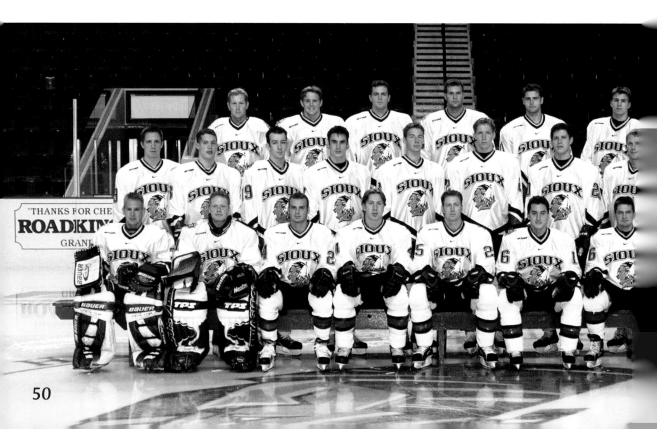

The University of North Dakota usually has a good hockey team. Many North Dakotans also pay close attention to high school sports.

Festivals and Attractions

Festivals in North Dakota celebrate the state's different ethnic heritages. Each year, Minot holds the Norsk Høstfest (HOOST-fest). This Scandinavian festival has traditional food, music, and crafts. The Norsk Høstfest is the largest Scandinavian festival in North America.

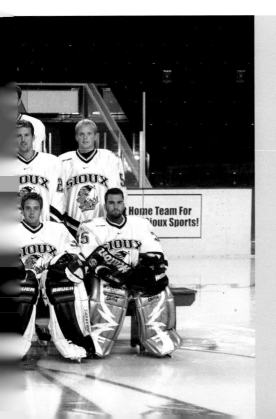

Since 1959, the University of North Dakota Sioux hockey team has won the NCAA Division I championship seven times.

Medora

A Frenchman named the Marquis de Mores founded the town of Medora in 1883. He named the town after his wife. De Mores started several businesses in Medora, including a meatpacking plant, a stagecoach line, and cattle and sheep ranches. In 1886, his businesses failed. De Mores moved back to France.

Today, Medora has been restored to look like an old west town. Several museums offer exhibits of local history. The Medora Musical, held every summer, highlights historical happenings of the area. Tourists can also visit the Chateau de Mores, a mansion built by de Mores. The Harold Schafer Interpretive Center tells about the history of Medora.

Powwows celebrate the American Indian heritage of the state. The United Tribes International Powwow, held in Bismarck each year, is one of the largest powwows in the state. It represents more than 70 Indian tribes. More than 20,000 people watch traditional dancing and drumming contests at the powwow each year.

In Medora, the Medora Musical highlights the heritage of western North Dakota. Performers sing and dance. They often reenact the Battle of San Juan Hill, fought by Theodore Roosevelt's Rough Riders.

North Dakota's people are friendly and know their neighbors. The state's low crime rate makes it a safe place to raise families. North Dakota is known for its rich history and hardworking people. Scandinavian festivals, powwows, and western culture are just some of the things that make North Dakota unique.

Children wear colorful regalia while they dance at the United Tribes International Powwow in Bismarck.

Recipe: Rhubarb Upside-Down Cake

Rhubarb is a vegetable that grows well in North Dakota. Rhubarb grows best in a cool, dry climate where the summers do not get too hot. Many North Dakotans have rhubarb patches in their yards and use rhubarb in dessert recipes.

Ingredients

4 cups (960 mL) washed and chopped rhubarb
1 cup (240 mL) sugar
1 box yellow cake mix
1 cup (240 mL) heavy whipping cream

Equipment

non-stick cooking spray
9- by 13-inch (23- by 33-centimeter) baking pan
2 mixing bowls
dry-ingredient measuring cups
liquid measuring cup
mixing spoon
colander
oven mitts

What You Do

1. Preheat oven to 350°F (180°C).

2. Spray the bottom of the baking pan with non-stick cooking spray. Set aside.

3. In mixing bowl, stir together chopped rhubarb and sugar.

4. Follow instructions on cake mix box to mix yellow cake in second mixing bowl.

5. Pour cake batter into the baking pan.

6. Using the colander, drain the extra liquid from the rhubarb mixture.

7. Pour the rhubarb mixture over the cake batter.

8. Pour the whipping cream over the rhubarb.

9. Bake for 40 to 50 minutes. After 40 minutes, check cake often to make sure it does not burn.

10. Remove cake from oven with oven mitts when top is golden brown.

Makes 12 to 16 servings

North Dakota's Flag and Seal

North Dakota's Flag

North Dakota's flag was adopted on March 3, 1911. It is similar to the flag carried by the North Dakota infantry in the Spanish-American War (1898). The only addition was the state name in a scroll at the bottom. The eagle on the flag stands for strength. It holds an olive branch for peace and arrows for war. Thirteen stars above the eagle stand for the first 13 states.

North Dakota's State Seal

North Dakota's seal was adopted in 1889. It reflects important parts of the state's history. Bundles of wheat, one of the state's main crops, surround an oak tree. The 42 stars over the tree stand for the number of states that were part of the nation in 1889. An American Indian hunting a buffalo represents the state's native people. The state motto, "Liberty and Union, Now and Forever, One and Inseparable," appears on the seal.

Almanac

General Facts

Nickname: Peace Garden State

Population: 642,200 (U.S. Census 2000)
Population rank: 47th

Capital: Bismarck

Largest cities: Fargo, Bismarck, Grand Forks, Minot, Mandan

Agricultural products: Wheat, sugar beets, potatoes, soybeans, sunflowers, milk, barley, flaxseed, beef, wool

Agriculture

Average summer temperature: 66 degrees Fahrenheit (19 degrees Celsius)

Average winter temperature: 10 degrees Fahrenheit (minus 12 degrees Celsius)

Average annual precipitation: 17 inches (43 centimeters)

Climate

Area: 70,704 square miles (183,123 square kilometers)
Size rank: 17th

Highest point: White Butte, 3,506 feet (1,069 meters) above sea level

Lowest point: Red River of the North, near Pembina, 750 feet (229 meters) above sea level

Geography

Western meadowlark

Wild prairie rose

Beverage: Milk

Bird: Western meadowlark

Dance: Square dance

Fish: Northern pike

Flower: Wild prairie rose

Fossil: Teredo petrified wood

Economy

Natural resources: Coal, natural gas, clay

Types of industry: Food processing, machinery, mining, tourism

Symbols

Grass: Western wheatgrass

March: "Flickertail March," by James D. Ployhar

Song: "North Dakota Hymn," words by James W. Foley and music by Dr. C. S. Putnam

Tree: American elm

First governor: John Miller, 1889–1891

Statehood: November 2, 1889; 39th state

U.S. Representatives: 1

U.S. Senators: 2

U.S. electoral votes: 3

Counties: 53

Government

Timeline

State History

1738
French explorer Pierre La Vérendrye visits Mandan villages in the Missouri River area.

1300s–1600s
Mandan Indians live in the area that is now North Dakota.

1804–1805
Members of the Lewis and Clark Expedition spend the winter at Fort Mandan.

1861
Dakota Territory is created.

1889
North Dakota becomes a state on November 2.

1880s
Bonanza farms become common in the Red River Valley.

U.S. History

1620
Pilgrims establish Massachusetts Bay Colony.

1803
Thomas Jefferson purchases the Louisiana Territory from France.

1861–1865
Union states fight Confederate states in the Civil War.

1775–1783
American colonies fight for independence from Great Britain in the Revolutionary War.

Greetings from
NORTH DAKOTA
2002

1953
Workers finish building the Garrison Dam on the Missouri River.

1972
The United States makes a deal to sell grain to the Soviet Union, creating good prices for North Dakota farmers.

1997
The Red River floods, causing the loss of homes and the evacuation of Grand Forks.

1916
Nonpartisan League candidates win elections for almost every state office.

1988
North Dakota suffers a severe drought.

1929–1939
The United States experiences the Great Depression.

1964
U.S. Congress passes the Civil Rights Act, which makes discrimination illegal.

1914–1918
World War I is fought; the United States enters the war in 1917.

1939–1945
World War II is fought; the United States enters the war in 1941.

2001
Terrorists attack the Pentagon and the World Trade Center on September 11.

Words to Know

blizzard (BLIZ-urd)—a heavy snowstorm with strong winds

escarpment (ih-SCARP-ment)—a long, steep slope that separates two level or more gently sloping surfaces

hydroelectric power (hye-droh-e-LEK-trik POU-ur)—energy that is produced by flowing water; hydroelectric power plants are often built at dams.

immigrant (IM-uh-gruhnt)—someone who comes from another country to live in a new one

initiative (ih-NIH-shuh-tiv)—the power to propose a law to the legislature by petition

interpreter (in-TUR-prit-uhr)—someone who can tell others what is said in another language

recall (REE-kawl)—the power to ask for a new election to remove elected officials

referendum (rehf-er-EHN-duhm)—a public vote on an issue or law proposed by the government

slough (SLEW)—a shallow indentation in the land filled with water; sloughs were formed by glaciers and are also called prairie potholes.

To Learn More

Coombs, Karen Mueller. *Children of the Dust Days.* Picture the American Past. Minneapolis: Carolrhoda Books, 2000.

Fontes, Justine, and Ron Fontes. *North Dakota, The Peace Garden State.* World Almanac Library of the States. Milwaukee: World Almanac, 2003.

Gunderson, Mary. *Cooking on the Lewis and Clark Expedition.* Exploring History through Simple Recipes. Mankato, Minn.: Blue Earth Books, 2000.

Silverman, Robin Landew. *North Dakota.* From Sea to Shining Sea. New York: Children's Press, 2003.

Internet Sites

Do you want to find out more about North Dakota?
Let FactHound, our fact-finding hound dog, do the research for you.

Here's how:
1) Visit ***http://www.facthound.com***
2) Type in the **Book ID** number:
   0736821910
3) Click on **FETCH IT**.

FactHound will fetch Internet sites picked by our editors just for you!

Places to Write and Visit

Governor's Office
Department 101
600 East Boulevard Avenue
Bismarck, ND 58505-0001

International Peace Garden
Rural Route 1, Box 116
Dunseith, ND 58329

North Dakota Tourism Division
400 East Broadway, Suite 50
Bismarck, ND 58501

State Historical Society of North Dakota
612 East Boulevard Avenue
Bismarck, ND 58505-0830

Theodore Roosevelt National Park
P.O. Box 7
Medora, ND 58654

Visitors to Medora can eat dinner at the Pitchfork Fondue, where steaks are cooked on the end of a pitchfork.

Index